Dear Parent:
Your child's love of reading starts here!

Every child learns to read in a different way and at his or her own speed. Some go back and forth between reading levels and read favorite books again and again. Others read through each level in order. You can help your young reader improve and become more confident by encouraging his or her own interests and abilities. From books your child reads with you to the first books he or she reads alone, there are I Can Read Books for every stage of reading:

SHARED READING
Basic language, word repetition, and whimsical illustrations, ideal for sharing with your emergent reader

BEGINNING READING
Short sentences, familiar words, and simple concepts for children eager to read on their own

READING WITH HELP
Engaging stories, longer sentences, and language play for developing readers

READING ALONE
Complex plots, challenging vocabulary, and high-interest topics for the independent reader

ADVANCED READING
Short paragraphs, chapters, and exciting themes for the perfect bridge to chapter books

I Can Read Books have introduced children to the joy of reading since 1957. Featuring award-winning authors and illustrators and a fabulous cast of beloved characters, I Can Read Books set the standard for beginning readers.

A lifetime of discovery begins with the magical words **"I Can Read!"**

Visit www.icanread.com for information
on enriching your child's reading experience.

For Tully
—L.D.

To my dad, the most dedicated and
loving veterinarian I know.
—C.E.

I Can Read Book® is a trademark of HarperCollins Publishers.

I Want to Be a Veterinarian Copyright © 2018 by HarperCollins Publishers. All rights reserved. Manufactured in China.
No part of this book may be used or reproduced in any manner whatsoever without written permission except in the case of
brief quotations embodied in critical articles and reviews. For information address HarperCollins Children's Books,
a division of HarperCollins Publishers, 195 Broadway, New York, NY 10007.
www.icanread.com

Library of Congress Control Number: 2018933322
ISBN 978-0-06-243247-6 (trade bdg.)—ISBN 978-0-06-243261-2 (pbk.)

Book design by Celeste Knudsen
19 20 21 22 SCP 10 9 8 7 6 5   ❖   First Edition

I Can Read!

BEGINNING
1
READING

I Want to Be a
Veterinarian

by Laura Driscoll

illustrated by Catalina Echeverri

HARPER

An Imprint of HarperCollinsPublishers

Dad and I are waiting to see
the veterinarian—or animal doctor.

We brought our dog, Gus.

It is time for his checkup.

Soon Dr. Wells calls us
into the exam room.
She weighs Gus.

Dr. Wells looks into his eyes,
nose, and mouth.

She listens to his heart.

"Gus is one healthy dog!"

Dr. Wells says.

She is a great vet.

She is so friendly and gentle.

"I wish I could be a vet," I tell her.

"I love animals.

But I am allergic to cats."

Dr. Wells smiles.

"You don't have to be a pet vet," she says.

"There are many other kinds."

"Could it be?" I ask Gus
on the way home.
"Could *I* be a vet?"

The next day,

I am at my riding lesson.

I see a man

wrapping a horse's ankle.

"Are you a vet?" I ask him.

"Yes!" the man says.

I am a large-animal vet."

His patients are horses, pigs,

goats, and more!

Hmm, I think.

I am not allergic

to *any* of those!

On a class trip,

I see another type of vet.

We are at the aquarium.

There is a diver

in one of the tanks.

"She is an aquatic vet,"

my teacher tells us.

"She is feeding the fish."

17

Later, the vet
is at the touch tank.
She answers all our questions
about ocean life.

Over the summer,

my family visits a national park.

In the park is a wildlife rescue center.

It's like a hospital for wild animals

who are hurt or sick.

The vets here are called
wildlife veterinarians.
They treat and care for the birds
until they are well again.

Then they release the birds
back into the wild.
"This is the best part
of my job," the vet says.

In the fall, my scout troop
visits a dairy farm.
It is a large farm with many cows.
We meet a dairy-cow vet.

"I test them for disease," she says,
"and make sure they get good food.
Healthy cows make lots of good milk."

23

We get to taste some milk.

Mmmmm.

These cows must be
very healthy.

I learn so much about vets.

I learn there are vets
who work outside.
Other vets work inside in a lab.
They study animal health.

Some vets work in schools.

They teach others

who will become vets.

Some vets work in
big, busy animal hospitals.

SUNNY HILL
ANIMAL HOSPITAL

And some vets have
their own small offices—
like Dr. Wells.

I see her again

at Gus's next checkup.

I tell her all I have learned.

"So what kind of vet
do you want to be?"
Dr. Wells asks me.
I think it over.
Then—*achoo!*

The cat next to me

makes me sneeze.

"I don't know," I say.

"I'm glad I have a lot of choices!"

Meet the Veterinarians

Small-animal veterinarian
a veterinarian who takes care of pets like dogs or cats

Large-animal veterinarian
a veterinarian who takes care of large animals such as horses, cows, goats, and pigs

Aquatic veterinarian
a veterinarian who takes care of fish and other animals that live in water

Wildlife veterinarian
a veterinarian who takes care of wild animals who are hurt or sick

Laboratory veterinarian
a veterinarian who studies animal health

Professor of veterinary medicine
a veterinarian who teaches people how to be veterinarians